Pourquoi activer mon Code en ligne :

Selon mon édition, l'activation de mon Code
me permet d'accéder aux enrichissements suivants,
sur ordinateur, tablette et smartphone :

	CODE ÉDITION LIMITÉE*	CODE ÉDITION CLASSIQUE
Lettre d'actualité du Code	✓*	✓*
Accès aux codes officiels secs	✓	✓
Mise à jour en continu		✓
Liens vers la jurisprudence		✓
Accès aux commentaires et textes complémentaires		✓
Accès aux articles des revues Dalloz		✓

www.activation-dalloz.fr

La clé d'activation se trouve sous l'étiquette de couverture

* Disponible pour les titres suivants :
Code civil, Code de procédure civile, Code pénal, Code de procédure pénale, Code de commerce et Code du travail.

Notre innovation, c'est vous.
DALLOZ AVOCATS

Big SALADS

Seasonal salads for the whole family

THE AUSTRALIAN Women's Weekly

contents

No longer is the salad just a humble side; these big salads are substantial enough to be enjoyed as a main meal. There's plenty of favourites as well as some fresh, new combinations to try for yourself. Best served on a shared plate for a casual meal, the big salad will fill you up.

Editorial & Food Director

Pamela Clark

TRIPLE TESTED FOR YOUR SUCCESS EVERY TIME

Australian cup and spoon measurements are metric. A conversion chart appears on page 77.

Salad days

Salad is wonderfully versatile – it can be served as a starter, side dish, an impressive main meal and even a refreshing dessert. Salads offer a variety of textures, colours and flavours to a meal and are an easy way to ensure we get those all-important five servings of vegies each day.

The popularity of salads is evident from the increasing number of salad bars and the availability of ready-to-use salad ingredients in supermarkets. This greater availability of fresh and exotic ingredients has meant that salads have become more interesting and enticing than ever.

The leaves used for salads can range from iceberg, cos, butter lettuce and watercress to rocket and baby spinach leaves. It is essential to select well when you buy. The golden rule is to purchase in season, when the leaves are at their peak and, therefore, less expensive.

Thoroughly wash all salad leaves, whether they have been pre-washed or not. Dry well, preferably in a salad spinner, but a clean tea towel will also do the trick.

Colour, flavour and crunch can be added with vegetables like capsicum, corn, red onion and asparagus. Avocado, with its rich buttery flesh, is the perfect partner for a salad containing seafood, such as prawns, salmon or trout. Walnuts, almonds or pine nuts, roasted in the oven or frying pan, provide a delicious crunch when sprinkled on top of a salad.

STORAGE

Store lettuce and salad leaves in the crisper of the refrigerator. Herbs should be kept standing upright in a glass or jug half-filled with water and covered with a plastic bag. Tomatoes and avocados should always be kept at room temperature until fully ripe, as they will not ripen after chilling.

COOKING VEGETABLES FOR SALADS

There are some vegetables that go particularly well in salads: snow peas, sugar snap peas, asparagus, peas and beans. They should be blanched or very lightly boiled, steamed or cooked in the microwave until still crisp. Immediately drain the vegetables and refresh with cold water to prevent any further cooking and to ensure they retain their bright colour; dry well before adding to a salad.

Roasted vegetables make wonderful warm salads: pumpkin, potato, parsnip, carrot and onion are delicious teamed with fetta or goat's cheese. Beetroot, either roasted or canned, should always be added at the last minute; its rich beautiful colour doesn't look so striking when it has bled through the salad and turned everything pink.

DRESSINGS

Dressings can vary from vinaigrettes to rich and creamy sauces. Different kinds of salads require different dressings – a simple vinaigrette is best on elaborate salads, a sharp vinegary dressing is good on tomato salads and a creamy dressing is lovely on crisp or soft salad leaves. For a twist, use lemon or lime juice instead of vinegar or avocado instead of mayonnaise in creamy dressings.

HOW TO DRESS A SALAD

Avoid overdressing salads as this can drown out the other flavours. Just before serving, pour on about half as much dressing as you think you'll need then toss the salad. You can always add a little more but too much dressing and you'll end up with a puddle at the bottom of the bowl and a very soggy salad.

These summer fruits and vegetables are packed with antioxidants and will brighten any salad.

Tip The salad can be prepared several hours ahead; cook the haloumi and add the dressing just before serving.

haloumi and watermelon salad with za'atar chicken

- 4 x 200g (6½-ounce) chicken breast fillets
- 2 tablespoons za'atar
- 2 tablespoons olive oil

haloumi and watermelon salad

- 2 tablespoons red wine vinegar
- 2 tablespoons olive oil
- 1 clove garlic, crushed
- 1 teaspoon caster (superfine) sugar
- 2 x 180g (5½-ounce) packets haloumi cheese, torn
- 1 teaspoon za'atar
- 1 tablespoon olive oil, extra
- 800g (1½ pounds) seedless watermelon, chopped coarsely
- ¼ cup (75g) pitted kalamata olives, halved
- ½ cup loosely packed fresh mint leaves

1 Cut chicken in half lengthways. Place in a medium bowl with za'atar and oil; toss to coat.

2 Cook chicken on a heated grill plate (or grill or barbecue), in batches, over medium heat for 2 minutes each side or until cooked through.

3 Meanwhile, make haloumi and watermelon salad.

4 Serve sliced chicken with salad.

haloumi and watermelon salad Combine vinegar, oil, garlic and sugar in a large bowl. Combine haloumi, za'atar and extra oil in a small bowl. Heat a medium frying pan over high heat; cook haloumi for 2 minutes or until golden all over. Add haloumi to the large bowl with watermelon, olives and mint; toss gently to combine.

serves 4
prep + cook time 25 minutes
nutritional count per serving 46.9g total fat (15.2g saturated fat); 3155kJ (754 cal); 16.8g carbohydrate; 65.4g protein; 2.9g fibre

serves 4
prep + cook time 15 minutes
nutritional count per serving 22.5g total fat (4.1g saturated fat); 1360kJ (325 cal); 19g carbohydrate; 8.7g protein; 7g fibre

Tips Any flavoured pesto can be used in place of basil pesto. You will need a bunch of watercress that weighs about 350g (11 ounces).

greenest green salad

- **5 slices multi-grain bread (180g)**
- **150g (4½ ounces) green beans, trimmed**
- **170g (5½ ounces) asparagus, halved lengthways if large**
- **⅔ cup (80g) frozen peas**
- **1 medium ripe avocado (250g)**
- **2 tablespoons lemon juice**
- **½ cup (130g) basil pesto**
- **1 tablespoon water**
- **3 cups (90g) loosely packed trimmed watercress sprigs**

1 Preheat a grill plate (or grill or barbecue) over medium heat. Remove crusts from bread and tear into bite-sized pieces. Toast bread on the grill plate 1 minute or until golden.

2 Add beans to a medium saucepan of boiling salted water; boil, uncovered, about 1 minute. Add asparagus to the same pan; boil about 1½ minutes. Add peas; boil for a further 30 seconds or until bright green. Drain; place in a large bowl of iced water to cool. Drain well.

3 Cut avocado in half, remove seed. Squeeze flesh out of each half; drizzle with half the juice.

4 Place pesto in a large bowl; stir in water and remaining juice. Add bread, beans, asparagus and peas, then watercress; toss gently to coat. Season to taste.

5 Transfer salad to a serving platter; top with avocado.

roast pumpkin and chickpea salad

- 1.3kg (2¾ pounds) butternut pumpkin, peeled, chopped coarsely
- 1 tablespoon olive oil
- ¼ cup (35g) unsalted pistachios
- 400g (12½ ounces) canned chickpeas (garbanzo beans), rinsed, drained
- 1 small red onion (100g), sliced thinly
- 150g (4½ ounces) baby spinach leaves
- 1 tablespoon coarsely chopped fresh chives
- 100g (3 ounces) fetta cheese, crumbled

preserved lemon vinaigrette

- 1 clove garlic, crushed
- 2 teaspoons finely chopped preserved lemon rind
- 2 tablespoons olive oil
- 1½ tablespoons white wine vinegar

1 Preheat oven to 200°C/400°F.

2 Combine pumpkin and oil in a large baking dish; season. Roast for 15 minutes or until tender.

3 Meanwhile, place nuts on a baking tray; roast, in oven, about 3 minutes or until golden. Remove from tray immediately.

4 Make preserved lemon vinaigrette.

5 Place pumpkin in a large bowl with chickpeas, onion, spinach leaves and vinaigrette; toss gently to combine. Serve salad sprinkled with nuts, chives and cheese.

preserved lemon vinaigrette Place ingredients in a screw-top jar; shake well. Season to taste.

serves 4
prep + cook time 30 minutes
nutritional count per serving 35g total fat (8.1g saturated fat); 2231kJ (533 cal); 34.1g carbohydrate; 15.5g protein; 12.4g fibre

Tip To use preserved lemon rind, remove and discard the flesh, squeeze juice from rind, rinse rind well and chop finely.

tip Dressing and seeds can be prepared a day ahead; refrigerate dressing until required.

warm asian chicken salad with sesame dressing

- 2 teaspoons sesame seeds
- 2 teaspoons salt
- 1 clove garlic, bruised
- 4 fresh coriander (cilantro) stems
- 4 x 200g (6½-ounce) chicken breast fillets
- 1 medium butter (boston) lettuce
- 200g (6½ ounces) broccoli, cut into small florets
- 100g (3 ounces) snow peas
- 1 lebanese cucumber (130g), peeled, halved, sliced
- 2 trimmed celery sticks (200g), sliced thinly
- ½ small red onion (50g), sliced thinly

sesame dressing

- ⅓ cup (80ml) olive oil
- ¼ cup (60ml) white wine vinegar
- 1½ tablespoons salt-reduced soy sauce
- 1 teaspoon sesame oil
- 2 tablespoons caster (superfine) sugar

1 Make sesame dressing.
2 Dry-fry seeds in a medium deep frying pan, stirring, over medium heat, until seeds are toasted lightly. Remove from pan.
3 Half-fill same frying pan with water, add salt, garlic and coriander stems; bring to the boil. Add chicken; reduce heat to low. Cook, covered, in barely simmering water 10 minutes, or until chicken is just cooked through, turning halfway. Remove chicken from pan; cover, stand 5 minutes before slicing or pulling apart into pieces.
4 Meanwhile, place lettuce, broccoli, snow peas, cucumber, celery and onion in a large bowl; toss gently to combine.
5 Divide salad between bowls. Top with chicken, drizzle with dressing; sprinkle with seeds.

sesame dressing Place ingredients in a screw-top jar; shake well. While preparing the salad, shake the jar a few times to dissolve the sugar.

serves 4
prep + cook time 30 minutes
nutritional count per serving 23.8g total fat (4.2g saturated fat); 1976kJ (472 cal); 12.5g carbohydrate; 49.6g protein; 4.7g fibre

thai chicken, papaya and peanut salad

- 1½ cups (240g) coarsely shredded barbecued chicken
- ½ small green papaya (325g), grated coarsely
- ½ cup (75g) roasted peanuts, chopped coarsely
- 250g (8 ounces) shredded vegetable salad mix
- 75g (2½ ounces) baby salad mix
- 1 cup fresh coriander (cilantro) leaves
- ½ cup (125ml) asian-style salad dressing

1 Combine ingredients in a large bowl, toss gently to combine. Season to taste.

tips You will need about half a barbecued chicken for this recipe. Shredded vegetable salad mix contains carrot, beetroot and broccoli stem. It is found in the chilled lettuce section of supermarkets. You can use coarsely grated vegetables if salad mix is unavailable.

serves 4
prep time 20 minutes
nutritional count per serving 12g total fat (2.2g saturated fat); 1167kJ (279 cal); 14.8g carbohydrate; 25.2g protein; 5.9g fibre

dressings

sesame soy dressing

Place 1 teaspoon sesame oil, ¼ cup soy sauce, 1 tablespoon sweet chilli sauce and 2 tablespoons lime juice in a screw-top jar; shake well. Season to taste.

serving suggestion Serve with an asian noodle salad or chicken.

prep time 5 minutes **makes** ½ cup (125ml)
nutritional count per tablespoon
0.8g total fat (0.1g saturated fat); 79kJ (19 cal); 2g carbohydrate; 0.6g protein; 0.04g fibre

anchovy dressing

Combine 6 drained finely chopped anchovy fillets, 1 tablespoon drained rinsed finely chopped baby capers, 2 tablespoons olive oil, 2 teaspoons finely grated lemon rind, 1 teaspoon dijon mustard and 1 tablespoon red wine vinegar in a small bowl. Season to taste.

serving suggestion Serve with lamb and beef. It also goes well with beetroot.

prep time 5 minutes **makes** ⅓ cup (80ml)
nutritional count per tablespoon
9.7g total fat (1.6g saturated fat); 398kJ (95 cal); 0.4g carbohydrate; 1.6g protein; 0.2g fibre

mustard mayonaise

Combine ⅓ cup mayonnaise, 2 teaspoons wholegrain mustard and ¼ cup lemon juice in a small bowl. Season to taste.

serving suggestion Serve with burgers or beef.

prep time 5 minutes **makes** ½ cup (125ml)
nutritional count per tablespoon
4.4g total fat (0.5g saturated fat); 224kJ (54 cal); 3g carbohydrate; 0.3g protein; 0.1g fibre

chilli dressing

Place 2 tablespoons sweet chilli sauce, 2 tablespoons lime juice, 1 tablespoon fish sauce, 1 finely chopped fresh small red thai (serrano) chilli, and 1 tablespoon finely chopped fresh coriander (cilantro) in a screw-top jar; shake well. Season to taste.

serving suggestion Serve with seafood or chicken salads.

prep time 5 minutes **makes** ½ cup (125ml)
nutritional count per tablespoon
0.0g total fat (0.0g saturated fat); 74kJ (18 cal); 3.5g carbohydrate; 0.4g protein; 0.3g fibre

tips Serve this salad on a shared platter. Recipe can be prepared 8 hours ahead up to the end of step 4. You can substitute spiralli or fusilli for the pasta shells. You will need about 1 whole barbecued chicken and 2 bunches of watercress for this recipe.

chicken and watercress pasta salad

- **500g (1 pound) small pasta shells**
- **¾ cup (60g) flaked natural almonds**
- **180g (5½ ounces) green beans, trimmed, sliced diagonally**
- **2 cups (240g) frozen peas**
- **3 cups (480g) shredded barbecued chicken**
- **4 cups (200g) firmly packed watercress sprigs**
- **120g (4 ounces) fresh goat's cheese, crumbled**

lemon and watercress dressing

- **⅔ cup (160ml) extra virgin olive oil**
- **2 tablespoons white wine vinegar**
- **1 tablespoon lemon juice**
- **1 cup loosely packed fresh flat-leaf parsley leaves**
- **2 cups (100g) watercress sprigs**
- **2 tablespoons finely grated lemon rind**

1 Cook pasta in a large saucepan of boiling water for 1 minute less than packet instructions state or until pasta is slightly firmer than al dente. Drain; rinse under cold running water, drain.

2 Meanwhile, make lemon and watercress dressing.

3 Place almonds in a dry frying pan; cook over a medium heat, stirring constantly, until fragrant and just changed in colour. Remove from pan immediately, set aside.

4 Meanwhile, boil, steam or microwave beans and peas, separately, until vegetables are just tender. Drain; refresh in a bowl of iced water; drain and transfer to a large bowl.

5 Add chicken, pasta and watercress to bowl with vegetables; drizzle with dressing, toss well to combine. Divide salad among 24 x 1-cup containers; sprinkle each with toasted almonds and goat's cheese to serve.

lemon and watercress dressing Blend or process ingredients until smooth; season to taste.

serves 24
prep + cook time 30 minutes
nutritional count per serving 9.6g total fat (1.9g saturated fat); 737kJ (176 cal); 16.3g carbohydrate; 5g protein; 2.3g fibre

Tips You can use any firm, waxy potato, such as pontiac or desiree, for this salad. You will need about half a barbecued chicken for this recipe.

chicken and potato salad

- **750g (1½ pounds) kipfler (fingerling) potatoes, scrubbed, unpeeled**
- **1 cup (120g) frozen peas**
- **3 slices prosciutto (45g)**
- **⅓ cup (80ml) white wine vinegar**
- **¼ cup (60ml) extra virgin olive oil**
- **1½ cups (240g) coarsely shredded barbecued chicken**
- **1 cup loosely packed fresh small basil leaves**
- **½ cup loosely packed fresh mint leaves**
- **3 green onions (scallions), sliced thinly**
- **½ cup (75g) drained sun-dried tomatoes, halved lengthways**

1 Place potatoes in a large saucepan of cold salted water; bring to the boil. Boil for 15 minutes or until tender. Add peas to pan for the last minute of cooking time. Drain. Cut potatoes in half crossways, season to taste. Cover to keep warm.

2 Heat a medium frying pan over high heat; cook prosciutto for 1 minute each side, or until crisp. Drain on absorbent paper.

3 Combine vinegar and oil in a serving bowl; season. Add warm potatoes and peas; toss to coat in oil mixture. Add remaining ingredients; toss gently to combine.

serves 4
prep + cook time
25 minutes
nutritional count per serving 21.6g total fat (4.5g saturated fat); 1930kJ (461 cal); 32.4g carbohydrate; 28.4g protein; 8.8g fibre

serves 6
prep + cook time 1 hour
nutritional count per serving 23.1g total fat (4.7g saturated fat); 1619kJ (387 cal); 16.7g carbohydrate; 28.4g protein; 4.3g fibre

Tip Labne is available from delicatessens and some supermarkets.

warm chicken, labne and maple walnut salad

- **500g (1 pound) baby beetroot (beets)**
- **¼ cup (60ml) olive oil**
- **300g (9½ ounces) unpeeled pumpkin, cut into thin wedges**
- **¾ cup (75g) walnuts**
- **2 tablespoons maple syrup**
- **600g (1¼ pounds) chicken breast fillets**
- **1½ tablespoons sherry vinegar**
- **2 teaspoons wholegrain mustard**
- **1 teaspoon dijon mustard**
- **125g (4 ounces) mixed salad leaves**
- **100g (3 ounces) labne**

1 Preheat oven to 200°C/400°F.

2 Trim beetroot, leaving 2.5cm (1 inch) of stems attached; halve beetroot lengthways. Place in a baking dish; drizzle with 1 tablespoon of the oil. Bake 15 minutes.

3 Add pumpkin to beetroot, bake for a further 25 minutes or until vegetables are tender.

4 Meanwhile, place nuts on a baking paper-lined oven tray; drizzle with syrup. Bake for 10 minutes or until browned, stirring halfway through. Cool.

5 Preheat barbecue (or grill or grill plate) on high heat. Brush chicken with 2 teaspoons of the oil; season. Cook chicken about 7 minutes each side or until browned both sides and cooked through. Transfer to a plate; cover to keep warm. Stand 5 minutes.

6 Meanwhile, combine vinegar, mustards and remaining oil in a small bowl. Season to taste.

7 Slice chicken thickly. Arrange salad leaves on a serving platter; top with beetroot, pumpkin, nuts, chicken and labne. Drizzle salad with dressing.

fattoush with harissa-rubbed lamb

- 600g (1¼ pounds) lamb backstraps
- ¼ cup (75g) mild harissa sauce
- ¼ cup (60ml) olive oil
- 3 pitta pocket breads (255g)
- 3 medium tomatoes (450g) cut into wedges
- 1 large green capsicum (350g), sliced thickly
- 2 lebanese cucumbers (260g), halved, sliced thinly
- ½ cup coarsely chopped fresh mint
- 1 cup firmly packed fresh flat-leaf parsley leaves
- ¼ cup (60ml) lemon juice
- 1 clove garlic, crushed

1 Combine lamb and harissa in a medium bowl; rub harissa into lamb, stand for 10 minutes.

2 Heat 1 tablespoon of the oil in a large frying pan over medium heat; season lamb, cook for 10 minutes or until browned all over and cooked as desired, turning halfway. Cover to keep warm.

3 Meanwhile, preheat grill (broiler). Split pitta breads in half; grill both sides until browned lightly.

4 Combine remaining ingredients in a large bowl; season to taste. Break pitta into pieces over salad. Thickly slice lamb; serve fattoush topped with lamb.

serves 4
prep + cook time 30 minutes
nutritional count per serving 28.9g total fat (8.2g saturated fat); 2416kJ (578 cal); 36.7g carbohydrate; 39.6g protein; 6.4g fibre

Tips You will need about 3 lamb backstraps for this recipe. For a more intense flavour, marinate the lamb for 1 hour.

tangy beef salad

- **500g (1 pound) beef eye fillet**
- **2 teaspoons vegetable oil**
- **⅓ cup (80ml) lime juice**
- **¼ cup (60ml) fish sauce**
- **2 tablespoons caster (superfine) sugar**
- **2 cloves garlic, chopped finely**
- **10cm (4-inch) stick fresh lemon grass (20g), chopped finely**
- **1 fresh long red chilli, seeded, chopped finely**
- **1 medium carrot (120g)**
- **1 small red onion (100g), sliced thinly**
- **1 lebanese cucumber (130g), cut into matchsticks**
- **1 cup loosely packed fresh thai basil leaves**
- **1 cup loosely packed fresh mint leaves**
- **1 cup loosely packed fresh vietnamese mint leaves**
- **½ cup (70g) roasted peanuts, chopped coarsely**
- **2 tablespoons fried shallots**

1 Cut beef in half lengthways. Heat oil in a large frying pan over high heat; cook beef for 5 minutes each side or until browned well all over and cooked as desired. Remove from pan. Cover; rest 10 minutes. Slice beef thinly.

2 Combine juice, sauce and sugar in a large bowl until sugar dissolves. Stir in garlic, lemon grass and chilli; add sliced beef, then toss to coat. Cover; refrigerate 2 hours.

3 Using a vegetable peeler, slice carrot into thin ribbons. Place carrot in a large bowl with onion, cucumber and herbs; toss gently to combine.

4 Arrange carrot mixture on a platter; top with beef, peanuts and shallots.

serves 4
prep + cook time 40 minutes (+ refrigeration)
nutritional count per serving 33.5g total fat (9.8g saturated fat); 2466kJ (589 cal); 17.1g carbohydrate; 52.7g protein; 5.1g fibre

pork chipolata and risoni salad

- 375g (12 ounces) risoni pasta
- 1 tablespoon olive oil
- 360g (11½ ounces) pork chipolata sausages
- 200g (6½ ounces) button mushrooms, halved
- 1 small red onion (100g), sliced thinly
- ⅔ cup (160g) roasted red capsicum (bell pepper) strips
- 100g (3 ounces) baby rocket (arugula)
- ¼ cup loosely packed fresh flat-leaf parsley

lemon dressing

- ¼ cup (60ml) lemon juice
- 1 clove garlic, crushed
- ⅓ cup (80ml) olive oil

1 Cook pasta in a large saucepan of boiling water until tender; drain. Rinse under cold running water; drain.

2 Make lemon dressing.

3 Heat half the oil in a frying pan over medium heat; cook chipolatas, turning occasionally, for 10 minutes or until cooked through. Remove from pan; cover to keep warm. Heat remaining oil in same frying pan, increase heat to high; cook mushrooms, for 5 minutes or until browned.

4 Thickly slice chipolatas. Combine chipolatas with pasta, mushrooms, remaining ingredients and lemon dressing in a large bowl; toss to combine, season to taste.

lemon dressing Place ingredients in a screw-top jar; shake well. Season to taste.

tip For the best result, use the largest frying pan you have to cook the mushrooms. Cook them in a single layer over medium to high heat, without stirring, until they brown, then turn them over.

serves 6
prep + cook time
30 minutes
nutritional count per serving 22.3g total fat (8g saturated fat); 2024kJ (483 cal); 49g carbohydrate; 19.1g protein; 5g fibre

Tip The goat's cheese we used was marinated in a mixture of olive oil, garlic, thyme and chilli.

lamb fillet salad with green pesto dressing

- 8 lamb fillets (550g)
- 1 clove garlic, crushed
- 1 tablespoon olive oil
- 1 large zucchini (150g)
- 2 large roma (egg) tomatoes (180g), quartered
- 4 flat mushrooms (320g)
- 350g (11 ounces) baby rocket leaves (arugula)
- 2 tablespoons marinating oil from goat's cheese (below)
- ½ cup (100g) soft marinated goat's cheese (see tip)

green pesto dressing

- ½ cup (130g) baby spinach pesto
- ¼ cup (60ml) olive oil

serves 4
prep + cook time
25 minutes
nutritional count per serving 50.9g total fat (10g saturated fat); 2224kJ (536 cal); 6.9g carbohydrate; 11.7g protein; 3.8g fibre

1 Combine lamb, garlic and oil in a medium bowl.
2 Using a vegetable peeler or mandoline, thinly slice zucchini lengthways into ribbons.
3 Cook zucchini, tomato and mushrooms on a heated oiled grill plate (or grill or barbecue) until browned and just tender. Cover to keep warm.
4 Meanwhile, cook lamb on a heated oiled grill plate (or grill or barbecue) for 4 minutes each side or until cooked as desired. Cover; stand 5 minutes.
5 Make green pesto dressing.
6 Combine vegetables, rocket and reserved marinating oil in a large bowl. Season to taste.
7 Slice lamb. Divide vegetable mixture among serving bowls, top with lamb, crumbled cheese; and dressing.

green pesto dressing

Place ingredients in a screw-top jar; shake well to combine.

vinaigrettes

red wine mustard vinaigrette

Place ¼ cup olive oil, 2 tablespoons red wine vinegar, 1 tablespoon wholegrain mustard and 1 teaspoon caster (superfine) sugar in a screw-top jar; shake well. Season to taste.

serving suggestion Serve with beef, lamb, pork or chicken. It also goes well with grilled haloumi.

prep time 5 minutes **makes** ½ cup (125ml)
nutritional count per tablespoon
9.2g total fat (1.5g saturated fat); 365kJ (87 cal); 0.9g carbohydrate; 0.2g protein; 0.2g fibre

thyme vinaigrette

Place ¼ cup olive oil, ¼ cup white wine vinegar, 2 teaspoons fresh lemon thyme leaves, 2 cloves crushed garlic in a screw-top jar; shake well. Season to taste.

serving suggestion Serve with asparagus or beef, or as a salad dressing.

prep time 5 minutes **makes** ½ cup (125ml)
nutritional count per tablespoon
9.1g total fat (1.5g saturated fat); 351kJ (84 cal); 0.2g carbohydrate; 0.1g protein; 0.2g fibre

oregano vinaigrette

Place ⅓ cup olive oil, 2 tablespoons red wine vinegar, 1 clove crushed garlic and 1 tablespoon finely chopped fresh oregano in a screw-top jar; shake well. Season to taste.

serving suggestion Serve with grilled haloumi, goat's cheese or a greek salad.

prep time 5 minutes **makes** ½ cup (125ml)
nutritional count per tablespoon
12.1g total fat (1.9g saturated fat); 456kJ (109 cal); 0.1g carbohydrate; 0.0g protein; 0.1g fibre

rice wine vinaigrette

Place 2 tablespoons rice wine vinegar, 1 tablespoon olive oil, 2 teaspoons mirin and 1 teaspoon dijon mustard in a screw-top jar; shake well. Season to taste.

serving suggestion Serve with pork and potatoes.

prep time 5 minutes **makes** ⅓ cup (80ml)
nutritional count per tablespoon
4.6g total fat (0.7g saturated fat); 208kJ (50 cal); 1.3g carbohydrate; 0.1g protein; 0.1g fibre

warm pasta and lamb salad

- 8 lamb fillets (550g)
- ⅓ cup (80ml) lemon juice
- 2 tablespoons finely chopped fresh rosemary
- 1 tablespoon dry red wine
- 1 tablespoon sweet chilli sauce
- 1 teaspoon brown sugar
- 1 clove garlic, crushed
- 1 tablespoon olive oil
- 4 medium roma (egg) tomatoes (300g), quartered
- 350g (11 ounces) wholemeal spiral pasta
- ½ cup (125ml) salt-reduced beef stock
- 2 tablespoons coarsely chopped fresh flat-leaf parsley
- 500g (1 pound) spinach, trimmed, chopped coarsely

1 Combine lamb, juice, rosemary, wine, sauce, sugar, garlic and half the oil in a medium bowl. Cover, refrigerate 2 hours.

2 Preheat oven to 180°C/350°F.

3 Lightly grease an oven tray. Place tomato, in a single layer, on tray. Bake for 20 minutes or until soft.

4 Cook pasta in a large saucepan of boiling water until just tender; drain.

5 Meanwhile, drain lamb over a medium bowl; reserve marinade. Heat remaining oil in a medium frying pan over medium heat; cook lamb for 4 minutes or until browned and cooked as desired. Cover lamb; rest for 5 minutes, then slice thinly.

6 Add reserved marinade, stock and parsley to the same pan; bring to the boil.

7 Combine tomato, pasta, lamb, marinade mixture and spinach in a large bowl; season to taste.

Tips Substitute the lamb with chicken breast, if you prefer. Use any shape wholemeal pasta you like.

serves 4
prep + cook time
50 minutes (+ refrigeration)
nutritional count per serving 14.3g total fat (3.6g saturated fat); 2388kJ (571 cal); 59.7g carbohydrate; 42.7g protein; 12.1g fibre

serves 4
prep + cook time
30 minutes
nutritional count per serving 19.8g total fat (4.2g saturated fat); 1675kJ (400 cal); 22.5g carbohydrate; 30.5g protein; 5.5g fibre

spicy lamb salad

- **1 teaspoon each fennel and caraway seeds**
- **½ teaspoon dried chilli flakes**
- **420g (13½ ounces) lamb backstraps**
- **2 teaspoons olive oil**
- **1 clove garlic, crushed**
- **2 tablespoons olive oil, extra**
- **1 tablespoon lemon juice**
- **1 pitta pocket bread (75g)**
- **400g (12½ ounces) canned chickpeas (garbanzo beans), rinsed, drained**
- **150g (4½ ounces) baby spinach leaves**
- **1 cup loosely packed mint leaves**
- **4 red radishes (140g), sliced thinly**
- **2 shallots (50g), sliced thinly**

1 Rub spices all over lamb; season. Heat oil in a medium frying pan; cook lamb for 3 minutes each side or until browned and cooked as desired. Cover; stand 5 minutes, then slice thinly on the diagonal.

2 Meanwhile, combine garlic, extra oil and juice in a small bowl; season.

3 Cook pitta bread on a heated oiled grill plate (or grill or barbecue) over high heat for 30 seconds each side or until toasted; break into pieces.

4 Place lamb in a large serving dish with the bread, dressing and remaining ingredients; toss gently to combine.

tips You will need about 2 lamb backstraps (eye of loin) for this recipe. Rest a weight such as a saucepan on the pitta bread to achieve stronger grill marks.

warm pork and choy sum salad

- 800g (1½ pounds) pork tenderloin
- ⅓ cup (80ml) lime juice
- 1 teaspoon finely grated ginger
- 2 medium carrots (240g)
- cooking-oil spray
- 500g (1 pound) choy sum, chopped coarsely
- 2 tablespoons water
- ½ cup firmly packed fresh basil leaves
- 1 cup firmly packed fresh coriander (cilantro) leaves
- 4 green onions (scallions), sliced thinly on the diagonal

sweet chilli dressing

- 1 tablespoon fish sauce
- 1 tablespoon sweet chilli sauce
- 1 tablespoon lime juice
- 1 fresh small red thai (serrano) chilli, chopped finely

1 Place pork in a large bowl with juice and ginger; toss to combine.
2 Make sweet chilli dressing.
3 Using a vegetable peeler, slice carrots into thin ribbons.
4 Lightly spray a medium frying pan with oil; season pork, cook over medium heat for 4 minutes each side or until browned and cooked as desired. Remove from pan; cover to keep warm.
5 Add choy sum and water to same heated pan, increase heat to high; cook, stirring, for 1 minute or until choy sum is just wilted.
6 Meanwhile, thickly slice pork. Place choy sum, carrot, herbs and onion in a large bowl with dressing; toss gently. Serve pork with salad.

sweet chilli dressing

Place ingredients in a screw-top jar; shake well.

serves 4
prep + cook time 35 minutes
nutritional count per serving 5.1g total fat (1.6g saturated fat); 1120kJ (268 cal); 9.5g carbohydrate; 46.5g protein; 3.9g fibre

tips Any asian greens can be used in this recipe; try buk choy or gai lan (also known as chinese broccoli). Add some baby spinach leaves and cucumber ribbons to the salad or toss through cooked rice stick noodles.

Tip Use a julienne peeler to easily cut the green mango into matchsticks. Julienne peelers are available from kitchenware stores and Asian food stores.

crab and green mango salad

- 125g (4 ounces) bean thread vermicelli
- 2 small green mangoes (700g) cut into matchsticks
- 300g (9½ ounces) cooked crab meat, flaked
- 1 small red onion (100g) halved, sliced thinly
- 1 cup firmly packed watercress sprigs
- 1 cup firmly packed fresh coriander (cilantro) leaves
- ½ cup firmly packed fresh mint leaves
- 2 medium limes (180g), cut into cheeks

sweet chilli dressing

- ¼ cup (60ml) lime juice
- 2 tablespoons fish sauce
- 2 tablespoons sweet chilli sauce
- 1 tablespoon grated palm sugar

1 Place vermicelli in a medium heatproof bowl, cover with boiling water; stand for 10 minutes or until just tender. Drain. Rinse under cold water; drain well. Using kitchen scissors, cut vermicelli into random lengths.

2 Make sweet chilli dressing.

3 Place vermicelli and dressing in a large bowl with mango, crab meat, onion, watercress and herbs; toss gently to combine. Serve with lime.

sweet chilli dressing

Place ingredients in a screw-top jar; shake well.

serves 4
prep + cook time 30 minutes
nutritional count per serving 1g total fat (0.1g saturated fat); 662kJ (158 cal); 25g carbohydrate; 12g protein; 3g fibre

Tips Dressing can be made 3 days ahead; keep refrigerated. For a quicker version, use bottled caesar dressing. You will need about 1 whole barbecued chicken for this recipe.

chicken caesar salad

- **4 slices white bread (180g)**
- **2 tablespoons olive oil**
- **4 rindless bacon slices (260g), sliced thinly**
- **3 cups (480g) coarsely chopped barbecued chicken**
- **1 large cos (romaine) lettuce, trimmed, torn coarsely**
- **6 green onions (scallions), sliced thinly**
- **1 cup (80g) flaked parmesan**

caesar dressing

- **¾ cup (225g) whole-egg mayonnaise**
- **1 tablespoon lemon juice**
- **4 drained anchovy fillets, chopped finely**
- **3 teaspoons dijon mustard**
- **1 tablespoon water**

1 Preheat oven to 160°C/325°F.

2 Discard crusts from bread, cut bread into 2cm (¾-inch) squares; toss with oil in a medium bowl. Place croûtons, in a single layer, on an oven tray; toast in oven for 10 minutes or until golden brown.

3 Cook bacon in a small frying pan over medium heat, stirring 5 minutes or until browned and crisp. Drain on kitchen paper.

4 Make caesar dressing.

5 Combine half the chicken, half the bacon, half the croûtons and half the dressing in a large bowl with lettuce, half the onion and half the cheese; toss gently.

6 Divide salad between serving plates. Top with remaining chicken, bacon, croûtons, onion and cheese; drizzle with remaining dressing.

caesar dressing Blend ingredients until mixture is smooth, season to taste.

serves 4
prep + cook time 35 minutes
nutritional count per serving 53.5g total fat (13.8g saturated fat); 3595kJ (860 cal); 34.9g carbohydrate; 57.6g protein; 5.6g fibre

Tip Dressing can be made up to 2 days in advance, refrigerate until required.

beef and mixed sprout salad

- 2 teaspoons finely grated ginger
- 2 cloves garlic, crushed
- 1 tablespoon soy sauce
- 2 tablespoons olive oil
- 600g (1¼ pounds) beef rump steak
- 1 medium carrot (120g), grated coarsely
- ½ cup (20g) alfalfa sprouts
- ½ cup (25g) snow pea sprouts
- 250g (8 ounces) baby spinach leaves

soy lime dressing

- 2 tablespoons lime juice
- 1 tablespoon olive oil
- 1 tablespoon soy sauce

1 Combine ginger, garlic, sauce and half the oil in a medium bowl. Add beef; turn to coat in marinade. Stand for 10 minutes.

2 Cook beef on a heated oiled grill plate (or grill or barbecue) for 3 minutes each side or until cooked as desired. Cover; refrigerate 10 minutes.

3 Meanwhile, make soy lime dressing.

4 Cut cooled beef into thin strips. Serve beef strips with carrot, sprouts and spinach; drizzle with dressing. Accompany with lime cheeks, if you like.

soy lime dressing Place ingredients in a screw-top jar; shake well.

serves 4
prep + cook time 30 minutes
nutritional count per serving 28g total fat (7.5g saturated fat); 2012kJ (481 cal); 2.8g carbohydrate; 53g protein; 2.8g fibre

Store vegetables in the
crisper section of the refrigerator.
Wrap leafy greens in a damp clean
tea towel and place in a plastic bag
to retain freshness.

Tip Baby salad leaves are also sold as salad mix or gourmet salad mix; it is a mixture of assorted young lettuce and other green leaves. You can use your favourite salad greens.

pork, orange and coriander salad

- **440g (14 ounces) pork fillet**
- **2 tablespoons char siu sauce**
- **2 medium oranges (480g)**
- **1 fresh long green chilli, sliced thinly**
- **100g (3 ounces) snow pea sprouts**
- **100g (3 ounces) baby salad leaves**
- **½ cup loosely packed fresh coriander (cilantro) leaves**
- **⅓ cup (80ml) orange juice**
- **2 tablespoons olive oil**

serves 4
prep + cook time 30 minutes
nutritional count per serving 10.6g total fat (1.9g saturated fat); 1152kJ (275 cal); 16.3g carbohydrate; 26.7g protein; 3.7g fibre

1 Cut pork in half lengthways. Combine pork and sauce in a medium bowl. Stand for 10 minutes.

2 Cook pork on a heated oiled grill plate (or grill or barbecue) for 6 minutes each side or until cooked as desired. Remove from heat; cover to keep warm.

3 Meanwhile, segment oranges into a large bowl; add chilli, sprouts, salad leaves, coriander and combined juice and oil. Toss gently to combine.

4 Thinly slice the pork. Top salad with pork.

serves 4
prep + cook time
20 minutes
nutritional count per serving 36.9g total fat (11.5g saturated fat); 3187kJ (761 cal); 74.4g carbohydrate; 28.8g protein; 7.3g fibre

Tip *You may need only half a clove of garlic in the dressing depending on the strength of the garlic.*

chorizo, tomato and rocket pasta salad

- **375g (12 ounces) fettuccine**
- **¼ cup (40g) pine nuts**
- **1 cured chorizo sausage (170g), chopped coarsely**
- **1 clove garlic, crushed**
- **2 tablespoons extra virgin olive oil**
- **1½ tablespoons lemon juice**
- **250g (8 ounces) buffalo mozzarella, torn into small pieces**
- **½ cup (75g) drained sun-dried tomatoes in oil, halved**
- **100g (3 ounces) baby rocket leaves (arugula)**
- **½ cup (40g) flaked parmesan**

1 Cook pasta in a large saucepan of boiling water until just tender; drain.

2 Meanwhile, toast nuts in a dry medium frying pan, over high heat, stirring constantly, for 1 minute or until golden brown. Remove from pan immediately.

3 Cook chorizo in same pan over high heat until browned. Drain on absorbent paper.

4 To make dressing, combine garlic, oil and juice in a small bowl; season to taste.

5 Place pasta, nuts and chorizo in a large bowl with dressing, mozzarella, tomato and rocket; toss gently to combine. Season to taste. Serve pasta sprinkled with parmesan.

crunchy pea, prawn and avocado salad

- 750g (1½ pounds) cooked medium king prawns (shrimp)
- 150g (4½ ounces) sugar snap peas, trimmed
- 3 small avocados (600g), sliced thickly
- 2 cups (100g) snow pea sprouts

chive vinaigrette

- ¼ cup (60ml) white wine vinegar
- ¼ cup (60ml) olive oil
- ¼ cup finely chopped fresh chives

1 Make chive vinaigrette.
2 Shell and devein prawns leaving tails intact.
3 Boil, steam or microwave peas until just tender; drain, rinse under cold water, drain.
4 Combine peas in a large bowl with prawns, avocado, sprouts and vinaigrette; toss gently. Season to taste.

chive vinaigrette

Combine ingredients in a small bowl. Season to taste.

serves 4
prep + cook time 25 minutes
nutritional count per serving 38.2g total fat (7.2g saturated fat); 1998kJ (478 cal); 8.2g carbohydrate; 24.6g protein; 3.7g fibre

Tips Without the prawns, this salad would be a delicious side for barbecued beef, lamb or chicken. The recipe is best made close to serving.

Tip This herbed ricotta would be perfect served chilled at a picnic.

roast vegetable salad with herbed ricotta

- 500g (1 pound) baby beetroots (beets), trimmed
- 500g (1 pound) pumpkin, peeled, sliced thinly
- 1 tablespoon olive oil
- 200g (6½ ounces) rocket (arugula)
- ⅓ cup (35g) coarsely chopped roasted walnuts
- 1 tablespoon roasted pepitas (pumpkin seed kernels)

herbed ricotta

- 1 cup loosely packed fresh basil leaves
- ½ cup loosely packed fresh mint leaves
- ½ cup loosely packed fresh flat-leaf parsley leaves
- ⅓ cup (80ml) pouring cream
- 500g (1 pound) fresh ricotta
- 2 eggs, beaten lightly
- 1¼ cups (100g) finely grated parmesan

red wine vinegar dressing

- 2 tablespoons red wine vinegar
- 2 tablespoons olive oil
- 1 teaspoon dijon mustard

1 Preheat oven to 200°C/400°F. Oil an 8cm x 22.5cm (3¼-inch x 9-inch) loaf pan (base measurement); line base and sides with baking paper.

2 Place beetroot on an oven tray; bake for 45 minutes or until just tender. Wearing gloves, rub off stalks and skin from beetroot while still warm. Cool. Halve or quarter larger beetroot, if necessary.

3 Make herbed ricotta.

4 Place pumpkin on an oven tray; drizzle with oil, season. Bake 25 minutes or until just tender.

5 Make red wine vinegar dressing.

6 Arrange beetroot, pumpkin and rocket on a serving platter; top with sliced herbed ricotta, walnuts and pepitas. Just before serving, drizzle with dressing.

herbed ricotta Process herbs until finely chopped. Add cream and half the ricotta; process until smooth. Add egg, parmesan and remaining ricotta; process until just combined. Season. Spoon mixture into loaf pan. Bake for 30 minutes or until browned lightly. Cool in pan for 15 minutes.

red wine vinegar dressing Place ingredients in a screw-top jar; shake well. Season to taste.

serves 4
prep + cook time 1 hour 10 minutes
nutritional count per serving 48g total fat (19g saturated fat); 2795kJ (668 cal); 23.7g carbohydrate; 30.8g protein; 10g fibre

char-grilled prawn and corn salad

- 500g (1 pound) peeled green prawns, tails intact
- 2 cloves garlic, crushed
- 2 tablespoons lime juice
- ½ teaspoon ground cumin
- 1 teaspoon caster (superfine) sugar
- 1 tablespoon olive oil
- 2 trimmed corn cobs (500g)
- 20g (¾ ounce) butter, softened
- 2 tablespoons olive oil, extra
- 3 x 15cm (6-inch) corn tortillas, cut into thin strips
- 1 medium avocado (250g)
- ½ medium iceberg lettuce (120g), shredded finely
- 6 small radishes (100g), trimmed, sliced very thinly
- 1 cup loosely packed fresh coriander (cilantro) leaves

lime and green chilli dressing

- 2 tablespoons lime juice
- ¼ cup (60ml) olive oil
- 1 green chilli, seeded, chopped finely
- 1 clove garlic, crushed
- 1 teaspoon caster (superfine) sugar

1 Combine prawns, garlic, juice, cumin, sugar and oil in a large bowl. Cover; refrigerate 10 minutes.

2 Meanwhile, make lime and green chilli dressing.

3 Brush corn with butter; season. Cook corn on a heated oiled char-grill pan (or barbecue), turning, 10 minutes or until browned lightly and just tender. Using a sharp knife, cut corn kernels from cobs. Transfer to a small bowl; cover to keep warm.

4 Meanwhile, heat extra oil in a medium frying pan over medium heat; fry tortilla strips, in batches, stirring, for 2 minutes or until golden. Remove with a slotted spoon; drain on paper towel. Season with salt to taste.

5 Season prawn mixture; cook on a heated char-grill pan for 3 minutes, turning halfway, or until just cooked through.

6 Halve avocado; scoop flesh into a large bowl. Add lettuce, radish and three-quarters of the coriander; toss gently to combine. Arrange lettuce mixture on a platter; layer with prawns and corn, then drizzle with dressing.

7 Serve salad topped with tortilla strips and remaining coriander.

lime and green chilli dressing Place ingredients in a screw-top jar; shake well. Season to taste.

serves 4
prep + cook time 40 minutes
nutritional count per serving 44g total fat (9.6g saturated fat); 2621kJ (626 cal); 21g carbohydrate; 32g protein; 9.2g fibre

tips You will need about 4 limes for this recipe. Leave the seeds of the chilli in the dressing if you prefer heat. The tortilla strips can be made a day ahead; cool and store in an airtight container.

Tip Vietnamese salad dressing, or 'nuoc cham', is as much a dipping sauce as it is a dressing.

vietnamese chicken and mango salad

- 2 x 200g (6½-ounce) chicken breast fillets
- 2 cloves garlic, crushed
- 1 tablespoon coarsely chopped coriander (cilantro)
- 2 fresh small thai red (serrano) chillies, chopped finely
- 1 tablespoon oyster sauce
- 2 medium mangoes (860g)
- 2 green onions (scallions), sliced thinly
- 120g (4 ounces) packet salad mix leaves with cabbage and kale
- 1 cup loosely packed coriander (cilantro) leaves, extra
- 1 cup loosely packed mint leaves
- ½ cup loosely packed vietnamese mint leaves
- ¼ cup (60ml) vietnamese salad dressing

1 Cut chicken in half lengthways; place in a medium bowl with garlic, coriander, half the chilli, and sauce; mix well.

2 Cook chicken on a heated oiled grill plate (or grill or barbecue), for 10 minutes, or until cooked through, turning halfway. Cool; then slice chicken thinly.

3 Meanwhile, thinly slice mangoes. Combine mango, onion, salad leaves, herbs and dressing in a large bowl. Add chicken; toss gently to combine. Season to taste.

serves 4
prep + cook time 30 minutes
nutritional count per serving 2.3g total fat (0.6g saturated fat); 818kJ (195 cal); 16g carbohydrate; 25.3g protein; 4.1g fibre

dressings

greek-style dressing

Combine 3 cloves crushed garlic, ⅔ cup lemon juice, ¼ cup olive oil, 2 tablespoons fresh oregano leaves and 2 teaspoons fresh lemon thyme leaves in a small bowl. Season to taste.

serving suggestion Serve with lamb, beef, chicken, pork and seafood salads.

prep time 5 minutes **makes** 1 cup (250ml)
nutritional count per tablespoon
4.6g total fat (0.7g saturated fat); 189kJ (45 cal); 0.5g carbohydrate; 0.2g protein; 0.2g fibre

sweet chilli dressing

Combine ½ cup sweet chilli sauce, ¼ cup rice wine, 1 tablespoon soy sauce, 2 cloves crushed garlic, 1cm (½-inch) piece grated fresh ginger and 2 tablespoons finely chopped fresh coriander (cilantro) leaves in a small bowl. Season to taste.

serving suggestion Serve with beef and pork ribs.

prep time 5 minutes **makes** ¾ cup (180ml)
nutritional count per tablespoon
0.2g total fat (0.0g saturated fat); 152kJ (36 cal); 7g carbohydrate; 0.4g protein; 0.4g fibre

balsamic dressing

Combine ⅓ cup olive oil, 2 tablespoons balsamic vinegar and 1 clove crushed garlic in a small bowl. Season to taste.

serving suggestion Serve with salads containing lamb, beef and roasted vegetables.

prep time 5 minutes **makes** ½ cup (125ml)
nutritional count per tablespoon
12.1g total fat (1.9g saturated fat); 456kJ (109 cal); 0.1g carbohydrate; 0.0g protein; 0.1g fibre

lime dressing

Blend 1 tablespoon coarsely chopped fresh coriander (cilantro) root and stem, 5 cloves coarsely chopped garlic, 1 teaspoon black peppercorns, ½ cup lime juice, 1 tablespoon fish sauce, 1 tablespoon grated palm sugar and two 10cm (4-inch) sticks coarsely chopped fresh lemon grass until chopped finely. Season to taste.

serving suggestion Serve with seafood, chicken, beef, lamb or pork. It also goes well with asian-style salads.

prep time 10 minutes **makes** ¾ cup (180ml)
nutritional count per tablespoon
0.0g total fat (0.0g saturated fat); 75kJ (18 cal); 3.3g carbohydrate; 0.5g protein; 0.4g fibre

Tip The easiest way to remove seeds from a pomegranate is to cut it in half, then release the seeds in a large bowl of water. This way you won't get splattered with juice and the white pith will float.

grilled lamb salad

- ⅓ cup (100g) quince paste
- 1 tablespoon water
- 600g (1¼ pounds) lamb backstraps
- 1 medium red onion (170g), cut into wedges
- 2 lebanese cucumbers (260g), seeded, cut into 3cm (1¼-inch) lengths
- 250g (8 ounces) haloumi cheese, crumbled
- 1 cup fresh coriander (cilantro) leaves, torn
- 100g (3 ounces) mesclun
- ½ cup (75g) pomegranate seeds

lemon dressing

- ⅓ cup (80ml) extra virgin olive oil
- ¼ cup (60ml) lemon juice

1 Combine paste and the water in a small saucepan over medium heat; cook for 3 minutes, stirring, or until smooth and heated through.

2 Brush lamb with quince mixture. Cook lamb on a heated oiled grill plate (or grill or barbecue) for 3 minutes each side or until browned all over and cooked as desired. Cover; stand 10 minutes.

3 Make lemon dressing.

4 Combine onion, cucumber, haloumi, coriander, mesclun, seeds and half the dressing in a large bowl.

5 Slice lamb thinly. Combine in a small bowl with remaining dressing; toss to coat.

6 Serve salad topped with lamb.

lemon dressing Whisk ingredients in a small jug until combined. Season to taste.

serves 4
prep + cook time
20 minutes
nutritional count per serving 37.9g total fat (12.9g saturated fat); 2474kJ (591 cal); 13.1g carbohydrate; 48.2g protein; 4g fibre

serves 12
prep + cook time
25 minutes
nutritional count per serving 19.8g total fat (5.1g saturated fat); 1092kJ (260 cal); 12.4g carbohydrate; 7.4g protein; 1g fibre

tips Lemon-infused extra virgin olive oil is available from major supermarkets. Substitute regular extra virgin olive oil and ½ teaspoon finely grated lemon rind, if you prefer. Dressing can be prepared 8 hours ahead; store, covered, in the fridge.

heirloom tomato and mozzarella salad

- 2 x 125g (4 ounces) long sourdough bread rolls
- 1 clove garlic, halved
- ¼ cup (60ml) olive oil
- 850g (1¾ pounds) small heirloom tomatoes, halved and quartered
- 220g (7 ounces) buffalo mozzarella, torn into small pieces

basil and lemon dressing

- 1 clove garlic, crushed
- 1 cup firmly packed fresh basil leaves
- 1 teaspoon white (granulated) sugar
- ¼ cup (60ml) white balsamic vinegar
- ½ cup (125ml) lemon-infused extra virgin olive oil

1 Make basil and lemon dressing.

2 Cut bread into 5mm (¼-inch) thick slices; rub both sides with cut side of garlic; brush with oil. Cook on a hot grill pan (or toast under grill/broiler) until browned lightly.

3 Combine tomato, cheese, toast, any remaining oil and dressing in a large bowl; toss to combine. Divide salad among 12 x 1-cup containers; sprinkle over extra fresh small basil leaves to serve, if you like.

basil and lemon dressing

Blend or process ingredients until smooth; season to taste.

warm potato and smoked trout salad

- **750g (1½ pounds) kipfler (fingerling) potatoes, scrubbed, unpeeled**
- **1 tablespoon dijon mustard**
- **2 tablespoons red wine vinegar**
- **1 tablespoon finely chopped fresh dill**
- **¼ cup (60ml) olive oil**
- **300g (9½ ounces) whole hot smoked trout**
- **1 stalk celery (150g), trimmed, sliced thinly**
- **1 shallot (25g), sliced thinly**
- **150g (4½ ounces) mixed salad leaves**
- **1 tablespoon rinsed, drained baby capers**

1 Place potatoes in a medium saucepan; cover with water, season with salt. Bring to the boil; boil for 15 minutes or until tender. Drain. Cut into 2cm (¾-inch) slices.

2 Meanwhile, whisk mustard, vinegar and dill in a small bowl; gradually whisk in oil. Season to taste.

3 Place warm potatoes in a large serving bowl with mustard dressing; toss gently to coat.

4 Discard skin and bones from trout; flake into large chunks. Add trout to potatoes with celery, shallot, salad leaves and capers; toss gently to combine.

serves 4
prep + cook time 30 minutes
nutritional count per serving 18.3g total fat (3.2g saturated fat); 1467kJ (351 cal); 25g carbohydrate; 18.6g protein; 4.7g fibre

Tip Smoked salmon can be used instead of trout, if you prefer.

serves 4
prep + cook time
20 minutes
nutritional count per serving 7.1g total fat (4.2g saturated fat); 1184kJ (283 cal); 15.5g carbohydrate; 37g protein; 2.7g fibre

greek barbecued prawn salad

- ⅓ cup (80ml) lemon juice
- 1 tablespoon honey
- 4 cloves garlic, crushed
- ¼ teaspoon cayenne pepper
- 600g (1¼ pounds) peeled green prawns, tails intact
- ¼ cup (60ml) lemon juice, extra
- 1½ tablespoons honey, extra
- 100g (3 ounces) baby spinach leaves
- 1 small red onion (100g) sliced thinly
- 250g (8 ounces) cherry tomatoes, halved
- 1 tablespoon finely shredded fresh mint leaves
- 1 tablespoon finely shredded fresh basil leaves
- 100g (3 ounces) fetta, chopped coarsely

1 Combine juice, honey, garlic, pepper and prawns in a large bowl. Season.
2 Cook prawns, on a heated oiled grill plate (or barbecue or grill) for 3 minutes, turning halfway or until browned and just cooked through.
3 Meanwhile, combine extra juice and honey in a small jug, season to taste.
4 Combine prawns with remaining ingredients in a large bowl; drizzle with dressing, toss to combine. Season to taste.

tip Serve this salad with tzatziki, a Greek yoghurt dip made with cucumber, garlic and fresh mint. You can buy ready-made tzatziki in supermarkets and delicatessens.

fennel and preserved lemon salad with haloumi

- **250g (8 ounces) haloumi cheese, sliced thinly**
- **1 tablespoon finely chopped fresh coriander (cilantro)**
- **1 tablespoon olive oil**
- **1 tablespoon lemon juice**

fennel and preserved lemon salad

- **2 medium fennel bulbs (600g), sliced thinly**
- **1 medium avocado (250g), halved, chopped coarsely**
- **2 pieces preserved lemon rind (80g), rinsed, chopped finely**
- **1 tablespoon lemon juice**
- **2 tablespoons olive oil**
- **½ cup firmly packed fresh coriander (cilantro) leaves**

1 Make fennel and preserved lemon salad.
2 Combine haloumi, coriander, oil and juice in a small bowl. Heat a large frying pan over medium heat; cook haloumi for 2 minutes each side or until browned both sides.
3 Serve haloumi topped with salad.

fennel and preserved lemon salad Combine ingredients in a medium bowl; toss gently to combine. Season to taste.

tip Fennel can be eaten raw or cooked. It is made up of a white or pale green bulb from which closely-arranged stalks grow. The stalks are topped with feathery green leaves where flowers produce fennel seeds. The bulb, stalks, leaves and seeds are all edible.

serves 8
prep + cook time
25 minutes
nutritional count per serving 17.2g total fat (5.5g saturated fat); 811kJ (194 cal); 2.1g carbohydrate; 7.5g protein; 1.5g fibre

ASIAN GREENS a mix of baby buk choy, choy sum, gai lan and water spinach.

BASIL there are many types, but the most commonly used basil in cooking is sweet, or common, basil.

thai basil also known as horapa; has smallish leaves and a sweet licorice/aniseed taste.

BEANS

green also known as french or string beans; this long thin fresh bean is consumed in its entirety once cooked.

sprouts also known as bean shoots; tender new shoots of assorted beans and seeds including mung beans, soya beans, alfalfa and snow peas.

BEETROOT also known as red beets or beets; a firm, round root vegetable.

BREAD, PITTA wheat-flour bread also known as lebanese bread. Available in small pieces called pocket pitta.

BUK CHOY also known as bok choy, pak choi, chinese white cabbage or chinese chard; has a fresh, mild mustard taste. Baby buk choy, also known as pak kat farang or shanghai bok choy, is much smaller and more tender than buk choy.

CAPERS the grey-green buds of a warm climate shrub (usually Mediterranean); sold either dried and salted, or pickled in a vinegar brine. Baby capers are smaller, fuller-flavoured and more expensive than the full-sized ones. Capers should be rinsed well before using.

CAPSICUM also known as bell pepper or, simply, pepper. Comes in many colours: red, green, yellow, orange and purplish-black. Discard seeds and membranes before use.

CARAWAY SEEDS have a sweetly rich flavour; available in seed or ground form.

CHEESE

fetta a crumbly textured goat- or sheep-milk cheese having a sharp, salty taste. Ripened and stored in salted whey.

goat's made from goat's milk; has an earthy, strong taste. Available in soft, crumbly and firm textures, in various shapes and sizes, and sometimes rolled in ash or herbs.

haloumi has a semi-firm, spongy texture and very salty yet sweet flavour. Ripened and stored in salted whey, it holds its shape well when heated. Best eaten while still warm as it becomes rubbery when cool.

mozzarella soft, spun-curd cheese; has a low melting point and elasticity when heated.

parmesan also known as parmigiana; a hard, grainy cows-milk cheese.

ricotta a soft, white, sweet, cows-milk cheese having a slightly grainy texture.

CHICKPEAS also known as channa, garbanzos or hummus; an irregularly round, sandy-coloured legume.

CHILLI always use rubber gloves when seeding and chopping fresh chillies as they can burn your skin.

cayenne pepper extremely hot, long, thin-fleshed, dried red chilli, usually purchased ground; both arbol and guajillo chillies are the fresh sources for cayenne.

flakes also sold as crushed chilli; dehydrated deep-red extremely fine slices and whole seeds.

green any unripened chilli; also some particular varieties that are ripe when green, such as jalapeño, habanero, poblano or serrano.

long red available both fresh and dried; a generic term used for any moderately hot, long, thin chilli (6-8cm long).

red thai also known as "scuds"; tiny, hot and bright red in colour.

CHIVES related to the onion and leek; has a subtle onion flavour.

CHOY SUM also known as pakaukeo or flowering cabbage, a member of the buk choy family. Stems and leaves are both edible, steamed or stir-fried.

CORIANDER also known as pak chee, cilantro or chinese parsley; bright-green leafy herb with a pungent flavour. Both the stems and roots of coriander are used; wash well before using. Coriander seeds are also available but are no substitute for fresh coriander, as the taste is very different.

CUMIN also known as zeera or comino; has a spicy, nutty flavour. Available in seed, dried and ground forms.

DILL also known as dill weed; used fresh or dried, in seed form or ground. Has an anise/celery sweetness; its distinctive feathery, frond-like leaves are grassier and more subtle than the dried version or the seeds.

FENNEL also known as finocchio or anise; a firm, crisp, roundish vegetable about 8-12cm in diameter. The bulb has a slightly sweet, anise flavour but the leaves have a much stronger taste. Also the name given to dried seeds having a licorice flavour.

GAI LAN also called chinese broccoli, gai larn, kanah, gai lum and chinese kale; used more for its stems than its coarse leaves.

GINGER also known as green or root ginger; the thick gnarled root of a tropical plant.

KIPFLER POTATO small, finger-shaped potato with a nutty flavour.

LEBANESE CUCUMBER short, slender and thin-skinned. Probably the most popular variety because of its tender, edible skin, tiny, yielding seeds and sweet, fresh taste.

LEMON GRASS a tall, clumping, lemon-smelling and -tasting, sharp-edged grass; the white part of each stem is chopped and used in Asian cooking.

LETTUCE

butter small, round, loosely formed heads with a sweet flavour.

cos also known as romaine lettuce; the traditional caesar salad lettuce.

iceberg a heavy, firm lettuce with tightly packed leaves and a crisp texture.

MANGO, GREEN sour and crunchy green mangoes are immature fruit used in salads, salsas and curries.

MESCLUN also known as salad mix or gourmet salad mix; a mixture of assorted young lettuce and other green leaves, including baby spinach leaves, mizuna and curly endive.

MINT the most commonly used variety of mint is spearmint; it has pointed, bright-green leaves and a fresh flavour.

vietnamese mint not a mint but a pungent and peppery narrow-leafed member of the buckwheat family; also called cambodian mint or laksa leaf.

MIRIN a champagne-coloured cooking wine from Japan; made of glutinous rice and alcohol and used only for cooking. Do not confuse with drinking sake.

MUSHROOMS

button small, cultivated white mushrooms with a mild flavour.

flat large, flat mushrooms with a rich, earthy flavour. Sometimes misnamed field mushrooms, which are wild mushrooms.

MUSTARD

dijon a pale brown, fairly mild french mustard.

wholegrain also known as seeded. A french-style coarse-grain mustard made from crushed mustard seeds and dijon-style french mustard.

NOODLES

bean thread vermicelli also known as wun sen, made from extruded mung bean paste; also known as cellophane or glass noodles because they are transparent when cooked. White in colour (not off-white like rice vermicelli), very delicate and fine; available dried in various size bundles. Must be soaked to soften before use; using them deep-fried requires no pre-soaking.

rice stick dried noodles made from rice flour and water, available flat and wide or very thin (vermicelli). Should be soaked in boiling water to soften.

OLIVES, KALAMATA small, sharp-tasting brine-cured black olives.

ONIONS

green also known as scallion or, incorrectly, shallot; an immature onion picked before the bulb has formed, having a long, bright-green edible stalk.

red also known as spanish, red spanish or bermuda onion; a sweet-flavoured, large, purple-red onion.

shallots also called french shallots, golden shallots or eschalots; small, brown-skinned member of the onion family. Grows in tight clusters similar to garlic.

OREGANO a herb having a woody stalk with clumps of tiny, dark green leaves with a pungent, peppery flavour. Can be used fresh or dried; also known as wild marjoram.

PAPAYA, GREEN unripe papaya; look for one that is hard and slightly shiny, proving it is freshly picked. Papaya will soften rapidly if not used within a day or two.

PARSLEY, FLAT-LEAF also known as continental or italian parsley.

PINE NUTS also known as pignoli; not, in fact, a nut but a small, cream-coloured kernel from pine cones.

POMEGRANATE native to the Middle East; a dark-red, leathery-skinned fruit filled with hundreds of seeds each wrapped in a lucent-crimson pulp having a unique tangy sweet-sour flavour.

PRESERVED LEMON a North African specialty; lemons are quartered and preserved in salt, lemon juice and water. To use, remove and discard pulp, squeeze juice from rind; rinse rind well then slice thinly.

RISONI also known as risi; small, rice-shaped pasta very similar to another small pasta, orzo.

ROCKET also known as arugula, rugula and rucola; a peppery-tasting green leaf. Baby rocket leaves (also known as wild rocket) are smaller and less peppery.

ROSEMARY pungent herb with long, thin pointy leaves; available fresh or dried.

SAUCES

char siu a Chinese barbecue sauce made from sugar, water, salt, fermented soybean paste, honey, soy sauce, malt syrup and spices.

fish also called nam pla or nuoc nam; made from pulverised salted fermented fish, most often anchovies. Has a pungent smell and strong taste. There are many versions of varying intensity, so use according to your taste.

harissa a Moroccan sauce or paste made from dried chillies, cumin, garlic, oil and caraway seeds.

oyster Asian in origin, this rich, brown sauce is made from oysters and their brine, cooked with salt and soy sauce, and thickened with starches.

soy also known as sieu; made from fermented soya beans. There are several variations; we use a mild Japanese variety unless otherwise indicated.

sweet chilli a mild sauce made from red chillies, sugar, garlic and vinegar.

SESAME SEEDS black and white are the most common of this small oval seed; there are also red and brown varieties.

SNOW PEAS also called mange tout (eat all).

SPINACH also known as english spinach and incorrectly, silver beet.

SUGAR, PALM also known as nam tan pip, jaggery, jawa or gula melaka; made from the sap of the sugar palm tree. Light brown to black in colour and usually sold in rock-hard cakes; the sugar of choice in Indian and most South-East Asian cooking. If unavailable, substitute with brown sugar.

SUGAR SNAP PEAS also known as honey snap peas; a fresh small pea that can be eaten whole, pod and all.

THYME a member of the mint family; there are many types of this herb but we most often use the "household" variety known as french thyme, or simply called thyme in most shops. It has tiny grey-green leaves that give off a pungent minty, light-lemon aroma.

lemon thyme a herb with a lemony scent, which is due to the high level of citral in its leaves – an oil also found in lemon, orange, verbena and lemon grass. The citrus scent is enhanced by crushing the leaves in your hands before using the herb.

TOMATOES

cherry also known as tiny tim or tom thumb tomatoes; small, round tomatoes.

roma also called plum or egg, these are smallish, oval-shaped tomatoes.

sun-dried tomato pieces that have been dried with salt; this dehydrates the tomato and concentrates the flavour. We use sun-dried tomatoes packaged in oil, unless otherwise specified.

ZA'ATAR a blend of whole roasted sesame seeds, sumac and crushed dried herbs.

ZUCCHINI also known as courgette; small, pale- or dark-green, yellow or white vegetable belonging to the squash family. Its young flowers are also edible.

conversion chart

measures

One Australian metric measuring cup holds approximately 250ml, one Australian metric tablespoon holds 20ml, one Australian metric teaspoon holds 5ml. The difference between one country's measuring cups and another's is within a 2- or 3-teaspoon variance, and will not affect your cooking results. North America, New Zealand and the United Kingdom use a 15ml tablespoon. All cup and spoon measurements are level. The most accurate way of measuring dry ingredients is to weigh them. When measuring liquids, use a clear glass or plastic jug with metric markings. We use large eggs with an average weight of 60g.

dry measures

METRIC	IMPERIAL
15g	½oz
30g	1oz
60g	2oz
90g	3oz
125g	4oz (¼lb)
155g	5oz
185g	6oz
220g	7oz
250g	8oz (½lb)
280g	9oz
315g	10oz
345g	11oz
375g	12oz (¾lb)
410g	13oz
440g	14oz
470g	15oz
500g	16oz (1lb)
750g	24oz (1½lb)
1kg	32oz (2lb)

liquid measures

METRIC	IMPERIAL
30ml	1 fluid oz
60ml	2 fluid oz
100ml	3 fluid oz
125ml	4 fluid oz
150ml	5 fluid oz
190ml	6 fluid oz
250ml	8 fluid oz
300ml	10 fluid oz
500ml	16 fluid oz
600ml	20 fluid oz
1000ml (1 litre)	1¾ pints

length measures

METRIC	IMPERIAL
3mm	⅛in
6mm	¼in
1cm	½in
2cm	¾in
2.5cm	1in
5cm	2in
6cm	2½in
8cm	3in
10cm	4in
13cm	5in
15cm	6in
18cm	7in
20cm	8in
23cm	9in
25cm	10in
28cm	11in
30cm	12in (1ft)

oven temperatures

These oven temperatures are only a guide for conventional ovens. For fan-forced ovens, check the manufacturer's manual.

	°C (CELSIUS)	°F (FAHRENHEIT)
Very slow	120	250
Slow	150	275-300
Moderately slow	160	325
Moderate	180	350-375
Moderately hot	200	400
Hot	220	425-450
Very hot	240	475

The imperial measurements used in these recipes are approximate only. Measurements for cake pans are approximate only. Using same-shaped cake pans of a similar size should not affect the outcome of your baking. We measure the inside top of the cake pan to determine sizes.

index